MW00413838

Strong for Performance

Create a Coaching Culture with Learning & Development Programs That Stick

Jeff,

With gratitude for you and your commitment to have a positive impact in the world!

Meredith Bell

Praise for *Strong for Performance*

"In *Strong for Performance*, Meredith Bell lays out a practical path for you to identify and then build a coaching culture that will benefit you and those you lead. You will see how you can create a safe environment by being honest with each other, providing both positive and constructive feedback as needed and resolve issues more quickly and have more time to be productive."
—**Garry Ridge**, Chairman and CEO, WD-40 Company

"*Strong for Performance* offers fresh perspectives and practical tools for overcoming the same problems that have plagued L&D professionals for years – achieving permanent, positive, behavior change in the workplace. Weaving personal anecdotes with data and inspirational quotes, Meredith Bell hits head-on the enablers and inhibitors for building new habits and creating real, lasting change. Whether you're responsible for the learning and development of a large corporation, or yourself, this book is a treasure chest for how to achieve maximum return on your time, energy and financial investment."
—**John F. Sullivan**, Senior Director, University of Virginia, Darden School of Business

"There are so many books that claim to describe how coaches can make a real difference in an organization, but with Meredith's book, she really delivers. Her writing and descriptions are concise and useful, and is as close to a practical guidebook for coaches as you'll ever find. I particularly appreciated how she dedicates a chapter to how all the components go together. It's a true resource for all coaches looking for a practical but effective resource in their work. This is one book I wholeheartedly recommend to my fellow coaches."
—**Maya Hu-Chan**, Author of *Saving Face: How to Preserve Dignity and Build Trust* and President, Global Leadership Associates

"Looking for a book that makes sense, feels like it will work and is *doable by you*? *Strong for Performance* is that book!"
—**Dr. Mark Goulston**, Author of *Just Listen* and *Get Out of Your Own Way*

"*Strong for Performance* uncovers why people often struggle with real needle-moving development, and provides a practical and humane remedy. The secret to long-lasting learning, Meredith explains, is to abandon conveying facts in isolation from relationships. Genuine, empathetic human connection with those more developed, with coworkers and team-members, with direct reports, and with oneself is necessary to reach developmental potential. *Strong for Performance* addresses development holistically, engaging the whole person. Meredith provides step-by-step guidance to empower people to coach themselves and others effectively for ongoing improvement, demonstrating both the "what" and the "how" to cultivate empathy and curiosity to catalyze real growth and development. Each chapter brings another element of how to bring cutting-edge learning and development and coaching practices together, with stories, concepts and real actions that naturally stick. As a coach, as a leader, and as a lifelong learner, I found so many insights worth framing and keeping in my regular sight for inspiration and accountability. Coaches, leaders, teams, and organizations who implement the principles in this book will be equipped to discover their personal and collective developmental capacity at levels otherwise unattainable."

—**MaryJo Burchard**, PhD, Founder & Lead Consultant, Concord Solutions, LLC

"*Strong for Performance*, unlike countless L&D writings, lasers in on the few, powerful levers for sustainable results and ROI. Meredith does not oversimplify neuropsychology and the hard work of behavior change and skill-building, but she does a marvelous job of demystifying it so we all are sure to benefit. She understands her audience—pragmatic, results-driven professionals—and offers an articulate, logical and, most importantly, executable guide. A must-read for anyone on the 'people' side of business accountable for long-term value creation."

—**John Reed**, PhD, MBA, MCEC, PCC, Managing Principal, Quinn Reed Associates

"Meredith Bell pulls back the curtain and shows what it takes to become the best—best leader, best talent developer, best all around. *Strong for Performance* breaks the mystery of what it takes to excel; offering tools, resources, and guidance that are easy to apply within any business setting. It answers the question I am often asked by my clients—*How do I go from good to great?* This book provides the answer."

—**Angela Cusack**, EdS, MCC, Principal, Igniting-Success

"In *Strong for Performance*, Meredith Bell provides impactful recommendations that are a must read for those of us who strive to invest in the development and performance of our staff and build a culture of feedback and coaching. This book is especially impactful for me on two fronts: My Business: I have a staff that I am charged with and honored to lead with a focus on perpetual development and top performance. My Clients: My firm helps our clients build cultures of alignment and productivity. The insights and recommendations that Meredith offers in this book are highly valuable for serving my company and my clients in the enhancement of learning and development programs to be more impactful and yield higher return on investment."

—**Steven D. Crawford**, Director & Senior Consultant, McGhee Productivity Solutions

"Meredith Bell is one of the most generous and empowering individuals I have had the pleasure of meeting. Her care for others and her commitment to give people the resources, insights and guidance needed to bring their best selves to their work and lives is evident in everything she does. That includes this book. Her passion for learning & development and coaching is reflected in these pages along with practical tools and resources to help organizations create a culture where people thrive."

—**Barbara Patterson**, Owner, Barbara Patterson International and Host, Real Business Real Lives Podcast

"*Strong for Performance* is a concisely and precisely written tool and resource that challenges assumptions and is, honestly, in-your-face about the facts. Written in the tone of a helpful guide, the book weaves real-life examples into concepts necessary for creating a coaching culture within an organization. Whether an organization is 4 people or 40,000-strong, the dynamics and results of a coaching culture are *undeniable*. As an expert in culture, I can say with absolute certainty that culture is the overriding factor that determines positive outcomes in societies, organizations, and families. Culture is the mental programming of a group of people; in *Strong for Performance*, Meredith helps us work on reprogramming our wiring so that we're more oriented towards growth, change, and success."

—**Kozhi Sidney Makai**, PhD, PsyD, Performance Psychologist

"This book is a treasure for any professional seeking to build a great culture, with great people, producing great results! Meredith provides a clear, practical and thorough system to create sustainable behavior change that's based on solid life experience and real hard science. She skillfully answers the question why most training programs make no improvement in job performance and cracks the code on bridging the gap between knowing and doing."

—**Ellen Cooperperson**, President/Chief Learning Officer, Cooperperson Performance Consulting

"Meredith Bell's *Strong for Performance* is a 'must read' playbook for learning and development professionals, professional coaches and executives who see the value of developing a coaching culture in their organization. Meredith's discussion about why many L & D programs fail to deliver results completely aligns with my many years of experience doing this work. More importantly, this book offers solutions for getting results and a return on our investments in people. What I appreciate the most about this book is that it offers practical tools to help learners hardwire new skills. My favorite that I use in my Executive Coaching practice is Focus-Action-Reflection (FAR)—a process for helping learners make progress on a weekly basis that works like compound interest over time. The subtitle of this book—*Create a Coaching Culture with Learning & Development Programs That Stick*—is the promise that it fulfills."

—**Mark Hinderliter**, PhD, Executive Coach

"While the world of talent development is rich with many fine books to build a learning leader's acumen and skill in developing people, finding a useful resource that shows how to concisely elevate the impact of learning and development programs by integrating multi-level and ongoing feedback, skill mastery, coaching,

and systemic enhancements, is challenging. Meredith Bell's *Strong for Performance* achieves just this in a practical and easy-to-apply manner, showing her understanding of both holistic talent development and the time constraints learning and development leaders have for building their own acumen while they educate and support the employees within the organizations they serve. The book is rich with encouraging mindset shifts, step-by-step guidance, and real-life examples that can help new and seasoned learning leaders create more integrated approaches to their development strategies and programs. In the world of talent development, the best approaches blend learning with ongoing support, feedback, and refinement during application. Meredith offers a roadmap to help learning leaders enhance their impact, so their learners can rise to greater performance, deeper professional fulfillment, and better business results."
  —**Sharon Weinberg**, MPA, ACC, CPCC, Leadership, Team Performance, and Business Strategy Coach

"We've all been there. We attend a great training and leave totally energized to put our new knowledge to work. But what happens next? Nothing! We go back to our old ways and the training is largely forgotten. What a waste! Meredith Bell fully diagnoses this issue and prescribes the solution in a way anyone can implement. Simply put, this book should be the first chapter in EVERY training book or curriculum! I can imagine no more valuable adjunct to any training than Meredith's 'transfer of training' concepts."
  —**Ben Hipps**, Founder, Keys2selling, LLC

"A concise resource for managers, leaders, and anyone else entrusted to develop others. Full of insights and concrete strategies for strengthening performance. Recommended!"
  —**Cory Richardson-Lauve**, Vice President, Nonprofit

"A number of years ago Daniel Pink, in his landmark book *Drive*, made the point that business has not kept up with what science tells us about motivation. Meredith Bell is showing, in a very practical, succinct way, that business also needs to pay attention to brain science if we want to help people really develop the skills needed in today's workplace. We have been on this journey with Meredith and her team for many years and can attest to its merits. Don't just read this powerful manifesto, apply it!"
  —**Rick Stamm**, Founder, The TEAM Approach

"*Strong for Performance* provides a rich source of knowledge, guidance, and experience for anybody involved in the important business of helping drive coaching in organizations. It offers a three-step process of Focus, Action, & Reflection. These three steps are the right ingredients in making any development program successful in changing behaviors, learning new skills, and mastering competencies that we can use to guide our thinking and actions in organizations. I

found this book to be very engaging. After reading the book, I take away a host of ideas and best practices that I will use in the business."
—**Shohreh Aftahi**, PhD, MBA, Chief Executive Officer, ThriveVance LLC

"Meredith's desire to help create a coaching culture is such a worthy contribution to the world of business, and I can see how this is a good time for having this conversation. During the few days as I was reading the book I met several of my clients who without a doubt would have benefitted from reading the book. It's such a powerful resource for anyone wanting to develop their business and team, and it's also a good reminder for leaders on what really drives good communication and follow-through. I especially enjoyed the parts about 3 Steps for Mastering Skills and Ongoing Focused Feedback. They allowed me to spot where my own potentials are in terms of creating lasting performance and results."
—**Adam Kawalec**, Life & Leadership Coach

"I love this book! Meredith Bell not only makes a case for why training rarely sticks, but offers solutions to make sure the learning lasts. Her straightforward strategies and case studies are incredibly helpful for anyone in coaching, consulting, or leadership. I just wish I'd had *Strong for Performance* when I started my coaching business!"
—**Libby Gill**, Executive Coach, Speaker and Author of *You Unstuck*

"*Strong for Performance* is the book every HR and Training Development professional, who is eager to improve the ROI for their training programmes, should read! It is short yet comprehensive with many examples of not just what the problem is in getting HR/Training more business aligned, but provides many great tips and strategies for ensuring your training is received, ingrained and acted upon by participants. My immediate action from reading the book—was to read it again!"
—**Graham Da Costa**, Chief Executive, Shine Feedback Ltd

"In this book, author Meredith Bell exposes a disturbing truth when it comes to lack of ROI and performance improvement in the corporate arena. Meredith reveals how to create a coaching culture that breeds safety and enables employees to take reasonable risks, make mistakes, and feel supported by all levels of management. I highly recommend, *Strong for Performance*. My take away from this read? Learning is one thing, implementation with follow-up is everything!"
—**Terry Earthwind Nichols**, Author of *Profiling for Profit: What crossed arms don't tell you...*

"Looking to learn how to transform *knowing* to *doing*? Meredith Bell's *Strong for Performance* provides us with a concise, detailed, and practical guide to accomplish short- and long-term measurable behavior change. At last we not only have a definition of the challenge, but also the solution. You are provided with the

knowledge and tools to facilitate the questioning and feedback process that will transform individual and organizational performance. Wow."
—**Kristin Ford Hinrichs**, Chief Effectiveness Officer, Best in Learning

"Meredith Bell has perfected the ability to present tactical coaching tools in a way that speaks to the hearts of readers. These 10 chapters provide a pathway to help individuals and teams create a coaching culture and all the treasures that come with it."
—**David Aduddell**, Author of *Breaking the Coaching Code* and CEO, Zoe Training and Consulting

"Meredith Bell generously shares her years of organizational work with clear principles to help any leader or professional be more effective in bringing change into their daily experience. She shares the "Why" behind the reasons we often don't make changes needed in order to be more of who we want to be! Meredith has spent her career building great tools to do this work easily and now she brings the How-To book to weave it all together!"
—**Jill Markle Hidaji**, Organizational Coach & HR Advisor, Hidaji Advisory

"Finally a book that understands the process of learning and change and how to make it happen."
—**Jeff Percival**, Entrepreneur, Author and Speaker, Percival Enterprises

"We all have fallen into the trap of hearing an insightful speaker and then letting regular life and old habits take over by the next day. Meredith explains why this happens and how to get from knowing something to doing something about it. She describes the power of creating a coaching culture in our workplace and why it matters. *Strong for Performance* is a must-read for anyone wanting to move from just saying they want a better work culture to creating and implementing a better work culture."
—**Katie R. Bishop**, Co-author of *The Best Seller*

"Meredith's book is the best I've seen in explaining development—360s, changing work habits, mastering skills, and coaching. It is straightforward, easy to read and understand, and practical. You can't help but learn from reading this book. I highly recommend it to experienced coaches, those who are on the receiving end of coaching, and those who are exploring becoming a coach."
—**Mark Spool**, PhD, President, Management Development Solutions

"Meredith Bell's *Strong for Performance* is an artful, story-based masterclass on how to launch learning that gets transferred into action and results. A must-read for any decision-maker who wants positive returns on their corporate training investments."
—**Dr. Pelè**, Bestselling Author and Host of the Profitable Happiness™ Podcast

"Meredith Bell's *Strong for Performance* is a guide designed to help organizations maximize the investments made in developing their people. Meredith shares her expertise in the field of leadership and performance by giving leaders and managers the roadmap they need to achieve performance with individuals and teams. As a leadership performance coach, I particularly enjoyed Meredith's compelling examples that touch the leader in all of us who are looking for ways to build capacity in their organizations. Everyone's time is valuable. These shared insights will help you experience a return on the investments you make in your talent."

—**Susan Conti**, Designing Leaders, Inc.

"As someone who has been a learning and development professional for 20 years, I found Meredith's concepts spot-on. They will help leaders to understand the importance of not only learning, but also applying what they have learned. The more we can work on ourselves, the better we make our environments around us. Meredith has tremendous experience in this arena, so her knowledge and expertise are needed for anyone who is looking for ways to improve."

—**Jill Joiner**, MS, MSOD, Leadership Development Specialist, MaineHealth

Strong for Performance

Create a Coaching Culture with Learning & Development Programs That Stick

Meredith M. Bell

First Summit Publishing

1st
Summit
Publishing

Strong for Performance: Create a Coaching Culture with Learning & Development Programs That Stick

Copyright © 2020 Meredith M. Bell

All rights reserved. No portion of this publication may be reproduced, distributed, scanned uploaded or transmitted in any form or by any means, or stored in a database or retrieval system, without the prior written permission of the publisher.

Please purchase only authorized electronic editions of this work and do not participate in or encourage piracy of copyrighted materials, electronically or otherwise. Your support of the author's rights is appreciated.

Printed in the United States of America
First Summit Publishing
An imprint of Performance Support Systems, Inc.
757-873-3700

Cover Design: Paula Schlauch
ISBN: 978-0-9850156-8-8

Dedication

For Lee, my husband and partner in life,
whose commitment, love and support are truly
the wind beneath my wings.

For every professional committed to creating emotionally
healthy cultures where people perform at high levels
because they communicate openly, care about and coach
each other.

Foreword

I've been in the business of coaching leaders for over 40 years, and more than 2,500 coaches in 55 countries have been certified in my Stakeholder Centered Coaching process. This approach uses a proven 8-step model for developing leaders and building teams: Ask, Listen, Think, Thank, Respond, Involve, Change, and Follow-up.

While our coaching practice is focused almost exclusively on leaders, we've discovered that coaching is actually needed at *all* levels of an organization. Coaching may start with C-suite executives, but best results happen when these executives cause coaching skills to cascade down to every manager, supervisor and team contributor.

In *Strong for Performance*, Meredith Bell explains how to create this kind of coaching culture.

She sets the stage by describing what's required for people to successfully adopt a new behavior pattern: they must literally rewire their brains. Current work habits have been in place for years, and it takes consistent reinforcement to replace old patterns with new ones. Practice and repetition are critical.

Meredith details all the elements you'll need to establish the type of coaching culture that ensures a better return-on-investment for your learning and development programs: 360 feedback, lots of practice, ongoing verbal feedback, coaching, and a support system. She also adds an important dimension that's often overlooked in developing a positive work environment: nurturing core strengths like courage, perseverance, composure, and self-confidence.

Meredith's book is based on more than three decades of experience working with leaders in organizations, first as a consultant and then as a publisher of assessment and development tools that have been used by thousands of organizations globally. She has seen first-hand the difference in the cultures or organizations where leaders model the coaching skills they want everyone to use in their day-to-day interactions with each other.

Very likely you'll identify with some of the stories Meredith shares, and you'll be encouraged to discover that lasting change and a healthy work environment *are* possible when you incorporate the recommendations she outlines here.

Use this book as a roadmap for strengthening the people in your organization and building a positive coaching culture.

Life is good!
Marshall Goldsmith
Author, *What Got You Here Won't Get You There*

Table of Contents

Introduction

In the 30-plus years my business partners and I have been in the corporate learning and development space–first as consultants and trainers, then as a software publisher of assessment and development tools–we've observed a disturbing truth:

Most programs designed to improve performance fall short of their goal. Most of the time there is no positive ROI.

If your training programs don't create long-term changes in behavior and improved performance, you may be pouring time and money down a hole. And you're not alone.

More than $150 *billion* dollars are spent each year on employee training. Yet it's estimated that *between 70% and 90% of this money is wasted*, because most of the participants don't apply what they learned back on the job.

I wrote this book to explain *why* this is the case (Part 1) and what you can do to create a coaching culture that ensures a better return-on-investment for your learning and development programs (Part 2).

By "coaching culture" I mean people at all levels who have the skills, confidence, and desire to help each other improve their ability to contribute to their team. In a coaching culture, everyone in the organization genuinely cares about the performance and well-being of every other person. People feel safe to take reasonable risks and make mistakes without suffering terrible consequences, because they know that others are committed to helping them succeed. Part 2 of the book describes the skills that make this type of culture possible.

Who the book is for

This book can be a valuable resource for three kinds of readers:

1. Both seasoned and fast-rising professionals with responsibility for the "people" side of the business: the *development* and *retention* of talent

2. Leaders and team contributors, for their own development

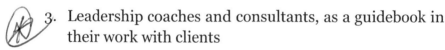

3. Leadership coaches and consultants, as a guidebook in their work with clients

You'll find it easier to apply the suggestions I describe if you work in an organization where executives are committed to:

- Investing in the development of leaders and employees

- Making ongoing and lasting improvements in performance

- Creating a culture of feedback and coaching

What you'll find here is based on my decades of experience working directly with hundreds of learning professionals, consultants and coaches who've shared with me their experiences as they've implemented our tools with clients.

This book isn't a long, academic treatise with footnotes. It's a brief, straightforward discussion about the realities every organization faces, along with science-based strategies for creating the kind of coaching culture that improves performance. My purpose is to equip you with a clear roadmap for reaching that destination.

My other book, *Connect with Your Team: Mastering the Top 10 Relationship Skills*, co-authored with Dennis E. Coates, Ph.D., is a learning support resource for leaders and their teams to improve the key interactive skills needed in a coaching culture:

Listen to Understand	Give Feedback
Guide Learning	Constructively
Coach People to Think	Accept Feedback Graciously
Get Buy-in for Expectations	Engage in Dialogue
Offer Encouragement	Resolve Conflict Creatively

Also, at the end of the book I've included: 1) a list of references about "transfer of training" challenges and 2) a description of tools we've created to support your work.

Note to the reader

Throughout most of the book, I use "you" instead of "they" when referring to changing habits and mastering new skills. This is intentional, because I'd like you to consider how this information applies to your own development, not just the leaders and team contributors in your organization.

PART 1

The Challenge

For decades, organizations have struggled, without much success, to deliver learning and development programs that have a long-term positive impact. In this section, you'll find out why this problem exists and what's needed to make sure your programs *do* improve the performance of leaders and teams over time.

"Most of the better training programs come in and blitz an organization with a lot of information and then they leave. The perception is that you received a lot of value, because you gained so much information. But without continuous follow-up, very little sticks from a one-shot training."

— Chet Holmes

The Ultimate Sales Machine

1

Why Most Learning & Development Programs Don't Improve Performance

A conversation I once had with an executive at a fast-growing start-up reveals why most organizations are not seeing a positive return on their investment in learning and development programs.

In his earlier career, "Bill" had been a manager and then an executive for 34 years with a Fortune 500 company. During those years he attended scores of classroom training programs on management and leadership. He reported that there had *never once* been follow-up after any of these programs. It was simply *assumed* that attendees would apply what they'd been taught. But after the programs, neither instructors nor participants' bosses followed up to see if the skills were being used back on the job. As Bill looked back over the three decades, he recognized that a lot of money had been spent with little or no return. He asserted that most of the training did *not* stick—with him or anyone else.

Unfortunately, Bill's experience isn't an isolated case. Often, after managers have attended an outstanding training program, there's an afterglow of good feelings about the instruction they received. They're eager and motivated to use what they learned. The assumption is that if the training is excellent and the participants buy into the content, they'll apply the skills after they leave the classroom.

But this rarely happens. All too often they revert back to what they've always done. After years of reinforcing existing work habits, their brains are literally hard-wired for those patterns; and the new skills haven't yet taken hold.

Even if participants wholeheartedly agree that the new way is better, when they're back on the job they get caught up in the work at hand. Most of the time, they don't make a conscious, consistent effort to apply the new skills, so the familiar habits kick in. The skills they learned in training aren't reinforced enough to establish new circuits in their brain. They don't "stick." This is why so many people get discouraged and give up trying. The time and money invested in learning and development doesn't transfer to improved performance on the job. *The reality is that learning events alone aren't enough to change behavior.*

Shocking Statistics

Experts in learning and development have been sounding the alarm about this situation for decades. Back in 1957, James Mosel published an article in *Personnel* where he cited "mounting evidence that shows that very often the training makes little or no difference in job behavior."

In an article in *Personnel* in 1988, Timothy Baldwin and Kevin Ford reviewed all the research to date about the transfer of training and concluded: "It is estimated that while American industries annually spend up to $100 billion on training and development, not more than 10% of these expenditures actually result in transfer to the job." This means *90% or $90 billion is wasted* because there's no discernible improvement in performance.

In the ensuing years, a stream of books from experts like Mary Broad, Jack Phillips, Donald and James Kirkpatrick and Roy Pollock affirmed the accuracy of this appalling number. Each attempted to offer varying solutions to the transfer of training issue. (See "References" for a bibliography.)

While most of the books assert that a structured program of follow-through is needed, none of them explains *why* this is the solution. Very few executives understand this issue and what's required to fix it. They don't appreciate that the role of training is to *introduce* the best practice, not to ingrain it as an automatic behavior pattern. That's why it's still rare for decision-makers to invest in an effective follow-up program. They don't understand that the real learning happens *after* classroom instruction is over. The confusion is compounded when executives are presented with development programs piecemeal and not as a complete system that makes it easy to understand how all the components are related.

The next chapter explains why reinforcement and practice are critical if you hope to get a positive return on your investment.

"Your former habits of thinking and being must disintegrate before better ways of behaving can begin to integrate...You need to clean out what no longer serves you before space is available for something even better to enter."

— Robin Sharma

The Leader Who Had No Title

2
Why It's Hard to Change a Work Habit

Has someone ever asked you to cross your arms the way you usually do, and then to cross them the opposite way? If you're like most people, you probably discovered the second position feels awkward and uncomfortable because *it's not your routine behavior.*

This experience is similar to what happens to participants in a training class when they're introduced to a new way of performing a skill such as listening. Even if they agree that the new approach is superior to their current one, they revert back to what they've always done when they're back on the job. After years of doing things the old way, these work habits are *literally hard-wired in their brains*, while the new skill isn't.

Most training doesn't have a lasting impact because...

KNOWING and DOING aren't the same thing.

Learning events can introduce the how-to. But *knowing* what to do—and even *wanting* to do it—doesn't mean someone will start using the skills when they return to their fast-paced day-to-day routine. The reason: *most behavior in a busy workplace is triggered automatically by ingrained habits and skills, not conscious decisions.*

Here's the reality:

> For an improvement in behavior to become a habit or skill, it must become hard-wired in the brain. This can happen only after many repetitions of the behavior through a lot of on-the-job application.

Every skill or habit is activated by a circuit of connected brain cells. Because the connection is physical, it's permanent. The cells in the circuit are even insulated, like wires. So it's not an exaggeration to say that a skill is hard-wired in your brain.

The hard-wiring serves you well most of the time. It makes performing a specific skill easy and automatic. You don't have to concentrate or ponder the action. It just kicks in when you encounter a familiar situation. For example, if you have to think about how you swing a baseball bat, you'll never get to first base.

Another value of skills: because they're hard-wired, they stay with you as long as you continue to use them. While you can improve a skill by remodeling the circuit, you'll never have to relearn it. You never forget how to swim or ride a bike.

Brain cells are stimulated to connect by your behavior. The more you repeat the behavior, the more the circuit will continue wiring, until it's fully connected and insulated. The problem is, some of the behavior patterns you established over the years no longer serve you well.

It would be nice if you could hit a "delete" key in your brain and erase the habits that get in your way—and simply replace them with the strengths you need. But that's not how your brain works. Hard-wired from years of programming, your brain doesn't distinguish effective behaviors from ineffective ones. It doesn't protect you from yourself. It doesn't say, *"Wait a minute! I can't establish a circuit for that, because it will cause problems down the road."* It will simply continue to reinforce the circuits for your actions each time you repeat them.

This is true whether you're working on your golf swing or interacting with the people on your team. This is why it's possible to end up with some self-defeating habits or less-than-effective skills, such as interrupting people when they're talking or procrastinating when faced with a difficult challenge.

From Dirt Road to Super-Highway

With most of the skills that matter, especially communication skills, establishing a new pattern can be challenging because the new pattern competes with an already-established pattern that has been hard-wired from years of use.

For a moment, think of a habit you have right now that's causing problems for you. A well-established pattern is like a familiar, well-traveled road. You know all the twists and turns, and you maneuver them automatically. But at some point you realize that the route you've been taking is actually slowing you down. So you decide to make a change and try something that works better. This is like trying to build a brand new super-highway. The construction is going to take time because you're starting with a dirt road. It's going to be an unfamiliar, bumpy, rough ride at first because the new behavior feels awkward. This means, when you try to change a habit, at first your results may get *worse* before they get better. Sometimes you'll forget what to do. Or you'll make mistakes. You can end up feeling disappointed and frustrated.

In order to get to that efficient road, you have to persist through the construction phase. You literally have to rewire your brain by creating new connections, and this takes time. It could be weeks or months, depending on the complexity of what you're trying to change and how often you put it into practice. Progress can be slow and uncomfortable. When setbacks happen, you'll be tempted to go back to the routine you know so well.

This is exactly what happens with many participants after training. Because a skill is new, they sometimes forget to use it, or they execute it awkwardly. When this happens in a fast-moving workplace, old habits kick in. These missteps are discouraging, creating a crucial moment in the learning process I call *the crunch point*.

The Crunch Point

When failures pile up, you might begin to think, *This is too hard. This isn't me. Maybe the old way isn't so bad after all.* You feel like giving up and going with what's already comfortable—your established habits. What you don't realize is that to get past the crunch point, what you have to do is *keep trying*—to persist in spite of mistakes and setbacks.

It takes a lot of repetitions to stimulate the construction of new brain circuits. If you stick with it, eventually the circuits will start to form, and your success rate will gradually improve. The skills will get easier. With consistent effort over the long haul, the new habits will replace the old ones, and the new behavior patterns will begin to kick in automatically. The question is: *What will keep you from giving up?*

You have to be willing to experience discomfort as you move from conscious competence—knowing what to do—to unconscious competence—being able to do it automatically. If you keep trying, eventually the brain cells connect and insulate. The new habit will get easier, and as it becomes dominant, you'll find yourself performing the new, improved skill without consciously deciding to do it. Your "failure rate" will approach zero.

A Personal Example

I attended a training event where the instructor asked us to perform a specific exercise for 30 days after we left the class. We were to write out a 2-sentence statement that he assigned and then, in the space below it, write our first and last names 10 times. Sounds simple, right? Until you consider there was a unique twist. We had to write all this with our *non-dominant hand*.

That exercise felt really strange at first. I didn't even know how to hold the pen in my right hand (I'm a natural lefty), much less use it to write. On those initial attempts, I experienced what many people do when they're trying to change from an existing habit to a new one. My penmanship, while terrible at first, got *even worse* the more times I wrote my name. As someone who takes pride in doing quality work, I was frustrated that I didn't see improvement and instead saw illegible writing between the first and last time I wrote my name.

Then I remembered something we all need to remember when we're attempting to change from our old way to a new way:

When you make a change, your performance often gets worse before it gets better.

This is because of the competition going on in your brain. Your familiar pattern has been established for a long time, and you perform the steps automatically, without having to think about them. This old pattern automatically kicks in as you're attempting to change to something else.

So I decided to relax and simply do my best each day, no matter how strange it felt or how long it took. Gradually, I noticed my right hand was more comfortable holding the pen, forming each letter, and writing out the words. By the end of the 30 days, there was a marked improvement in my penmanship.

In this particular case, the purpose of the exercise was *not* to permanently cease writing with my dominant hand. But when we're talking about learning to listen to others more deeply or allow them to finish their sentences without interrupting or responding graciously to constructive feedback, that's very different. In these instances, you *do* want to replace your current, less effective pattern with one that will serve you and others better. This means permanently rewiring your brain for the skill so the new way becomes *the* way you perform the skill.

How long does it take to rewire your brain?

The answer is that it depends on these conditions:

- **How much improvement you need.** If you only need a minor tweak to align with the best practice, fewer reps will be needed. If your old work habit needs an overhaul, it will probably take a lot more time.

- **How complex the skill is.** While a safety procedure may be simple, most interpersonal skills like engaging in dialogue tend to be complex.

- **How often you practice the skill.** If you only remember to do the skill once a week, establishing a better habit could take a year or more. If you make a conscious effort every day, you'll achieve success a lot quicker.

- **How motivated you are to change.** Making attempts to change in order to comply with another person's priorities rarely lasts, because feelings of resentment can creep in. When *you* can see and feel the benefit of making the change, you're more likely to make the long-term commitment required to stick with it until the new behavior becomes what you naturally do.

- **Whether you have coaching.** When you're trying to change a behavior pattern, you probably won't experience a lot of success at first. You'll know *what* to do. But because of your current, comfortable way of doing things, at first you'll tend to forget. You'll be moving fast, and you'll just do what you usually do. This high failure rate early on happens to everybody. It comes with the territory. It helps to have reminders, advice, feedback, accountability and encouragement, i.e., *coaching*. With coaching and persistence, your success rate will improve (see Chapter 7).

The next chapter describes the components needed to empower learning that sticks.

"Instead of utilizing merely a motivational speaker, make sure that you bring someone in who will provide usable tools that will lead to effective action. Make certain that your people learn to be bolder and more innovative. The solution is always daring decisions followed by daring action."

— Dusan Djukich

Straight-Line Leadership

3

How to Make Sure Your Training "Sticks"

You won't find one magic bullet that guarantees a positive ROI from your learning and development programs. However, there *is* a combination of elements that can increase the likelihood that you'll get better results than your programs are achieving now. The keys are to provide opportunities for repetition and practice and to establish a system for feedback, accountability, coaching and support.

The rest of this book describes each component in detail and how it fits into an overall system of reinforcement. Here's a brief summary of each:

Diagnostic 360 Feedback

It would be ideal if people in the workplace gave each other verbal feedback on a regular basis. Or if they would *ask* each of their stakeholders for feedback often. Unfortunately, most organizations don't have this kind of culture.

360 feedback is a technology that diagnoses strengths and opportunities for development in behavior and performance, so learning and development programs can be targeted to the

greatest need. Questionnaires collect data anonymously and confidentially, and reports identify areas of strength and opportunities for development.

3 Steps for Mastering Skills

There's a proven process for moving from awkward to automatic when applying a new skill. Most people aren't aware of these steps, so achieving mastery becomes more difficult or even impossible.

Learning how to complete three steps—focus, action and reflection—each time you practice a skill facilitates the brain's wiring of the new pattern. Repeating the steps is the other critical piece required to make the new work habit the default behavior.

Ongoing Focused Feedback

Diagnostic 360 feedback is the best way to identify strengths and areas that need improvement. But this initial effort is not enough. As you attempt to make changes, you also need ongoing focused feedback about your progress.

Learning how to ask for and receive focused feedback is critical to make it safe for others to tell you the truth about the effects of your words and actions.

Coaching

Making changes in behavior patterns is daunting. A coach can help you focus on what's important, keep you on track, encourage you, and hold you accountable. It's reassuring to have someone who challenges you to stretch outside your comfort zone and is in your corner during the tough times.

When effective coaching is provided at the executive level, you can create a cascade effect that helps to establish a coaching culture throughout the organization. In this environment, people at all levels have the skills needed to coach others, whether the relationship is boss, peer or direct report.

Support Systems

There's a reason why programs like Alcoholics Anonymous and Weight Watchers have been successful for so many decades. Their structure provides support for the participants, whether it's in the form of an individual sponsor or simply the energy and encouragement of the group.

A support system in the workplace can take different forms. They all serve the same purpose: to provide an environment that encourages, reinforces, and helps sustain the desired changes.

Core Strengths

If you incorporate all the above ingredients but ignore the importance of core strengths, your programs may fall short. Making the change from an established way of performing a skill to a new, unfamiliar one requires that you engage strengths like self-awareness, courage, commitment and effort.

Leaders and team members alike will need to engage these strengths in order to persist through the transition from awkward to automatic.

PART 2

The Solution

Attempting to implement just one idea won't work if your goal is to improve performance and build a culture where people coach each other. Instead, these elements must work together to produce the results you're looking for:

- 360 Feedback
- 3 Steps for Mastering Skills
- Focused Feedback
- Coaching
- Support Systems
- Core Strengths

"Confidential 360-degree feedback is the best way for successful people to identify what they need to improve in their relationships at work. If we can stop, listen, and think about what others are seeing in us, we have a great opportunity. We can compare the self that we want to be with the self that we are presenting to the rest of the world. We can then begin to make the real changes that are needed to close the gap between our stated values and our actual behavior."

— Marshall Goldsmith

What Got You Here Won't Get You There

4

Diagnostic 360 Feedback

Imagine if every leader in your organization—from executive to supervisor—regularly met with stakeholders to ask for feedback: *"What am I doing that you'd like to see me do more of? What would you like me to change or stop doing altogether?"* The benefit of this feedback is that they'd be able to target their efforts to improve.

Since most organizations don't have this kind of culture, technologies for collecting input from others were developed in the 1980s and are still in widespread use today. It's a formal, centralized process known as 360-degree feedback (or simply 360 feedback) that begins a rational approach to improving individual performance by:

1. Diagnosing strengths and opportunities for development

2. Providing targeted learning and development programs

3. Supporting coaching efforts to reinforce the new work habits

Many companies are just now beginning to implement 360 feedback as part of their commitment to leader and team development.

What Is 360 Feedback?

There's real power in hearing from your direct reports, peers and others who are impacted by your behavior at work. It's referred to as "360" feedback because you're getting input from many sources, typically individuals at all different levels in the organization. The idea behind 360 feedback is that other people with first-hand knowledge of your performance can give you valuable information about your strengths and opportunities for development.

The process focuses on observable behaviors related to competencies established for leaders and employees. Because reports combine scaled ratings from many sources, the data are as detailed and accurate as measurements of human performance can be. Most 360 technologies have extensive safeguards for anonymity and confidentiality to ensure that respondents feel safe about giving their honest opinions.

My Own Experience Receiving 360 Feedback

I remember the first time we used our 360 feedback software, *20/20 Insight GOLD*, in our own company to ask employees for input about each of the three owners. I wasn't sure what to expect since I'd never done this before. I got some excellent insights about my strengths, some of which I hadn't given myself credit for. But I also had a rude awakening when I read what people *didn't* like, especially one thing I did that caused problems for several employees. *This behavior was an absolute blind spot for me.*

I'm one of those people who likes to get focused on a task and not be interrupted. But back then I was not very effective at telling others when I was in "prime time" mode and not to be disturbed. So if someone came into my office, I'd look up and frown, giving the impression that I was annoyed with them. The result was that some people felt intimidated about approaching me and even avoided me. After studying my report, I apologized to the whole team for my behavior and resolved to be clearer about my prime time. I also made a commitment to give them a warmer welcome when they approached me. This made a big difference in my relationship with every person in our company.

What Are the Benefits? *OF 360 FEEDBACK?*

For many organizations, 360 feedback is the most effective and time-efficient way to give people information about hard-to-measure aspects of their performance.

- **Eliminate blind spots.** 360 feedback opens our eyes to behaviors we may not have been aware of previously. On the positive side, we have strengths others value and want us to use more often. On the other hand, we also say or do things that negatively impact others. We don't realize the problems our action is causing.

- **Feedback from many sources.** Feedback from one source is better than no feedback at all. But even when it's from the boss, it's still one person's opinion. Consistent feedback from many sources is more convincing and credible.

- **Data for individual development planning**. The wealth of objective feedback about a variety of competencies makes it easier to study the results and identify priority areas for improving.

- **Data for needs assessment and Human Resource Development planning.** When you aggregate data for individual feedback, you can identify skill strengths and deficits across groups and the entire organization.

Are You Ready for 360?

If 360 feedback is new to your organization—or if you've tried it in the past and had a bad initial experience—there are some common-sense steps you can take to ensure the process goes well and recipients receive honest, useful information.

Here are four areas to consider when evaluating the readiness of people to give *or* receive 360 feedback. Addressing these up-front will help you avoid issues around implementation due to lack of clarity and commitment.

1. **Feedback Climate**

   ✓ *Do people have confidence that their input will be anonymous and confidential?*

   ✓ *Is there an environment of trust where people feel safe about giving honest, fair ratings and comments without fear of reprisal?*

2. **Awareness and Acceptance**

   ✓ *Do recipients and respondents alike understand the purpose of 360 feedback and how it works?*

   ✓ *Are they open to the idea of giving and/or receiving this type of feedback?*

3. **Feedback Practices**

   ✓ *Are managers and team contributors already in the habit of asking for and giving each other verbal feedback (both positive and constructive)?*

   ✓ *Do managers and team contributors have the skills needed to provide helpful feedback?*

4. Development Practices

- ✓ *Does your organization support the professional development of leaders and team contributors?*

- ✓ *Are managers involved in helping members of their team create plans for development?*

Download the checklist, "Is Your Organization Ready for 360?" to discover the steps that ensure your 360 feedback process goes smoothly:
https://GrowStrongLeaders.com/Bonus

A Caution

360 feedback is meant to be a diagnostic tool for *development only*. Feedback recipients study the ratings and comments to identify strengths and areas for improvement. Then, with input from their manager, they create a plan for development, committing to take certain actions during a specified period of time.

In the early days, some companies were eager to replace their traditional performance appraisal process. They saw 360 feedback as an alternative. They believed they could use the scores from the reports to make compensation decisions. Not a good idea!

I recall one organization that used our software for this purpose, despite my strong warning not to do so. In year 1, respondents gave honest feedback. But in year 2, they realized the impact these ratings had on their co-workers' salary increases, so they started rating each other artificially high. The 360 process ceased to have any value as a development tool since the results were not an accurate reflection of the person's performance.

If your organization is new to 360 feedback, participants will give higher-quality, honest responses if you invest time up-front educating them about the process. This orientation ideally includes feedback recipients *and* feedback givers. Important points to cover include:

- How the assessment process will work

- What will be done to ensure all responses are confidential and anonymous

- Who will see the results

- How the results will be used for development

The Most Powerful Way to Use 360

A doctor's diagnosis can reveal the disease, but this information can't cure it. Likewise, 360 feedback can identify priority areas for improvement; but this input alone isn't enough to improve work habits.

As we explored in Part I, to achieve the desired changes in behavior, 360 feedback needs to lead to learning and development, followed by several months of practice, accompanied by ongoing coaching, feedback, and accountability. It takes that long for the brain cells to grow and reconnect into new pathways that are the physical basis for new behavior patterns.

The most powerful use of 360-degree feedback is to measure individual performance improvement.

Used in this way, 360 feedback works as a diagnostic assessment, a means for targeting developmental programs, and a way to check whether performance has improved over time. The concept is simple.

1. Administer a behavior-based 360 assessment.

2. Conduct behavior-based learning and development programs based on the results.

3. Follow up with ongoing coaching and reinforcement.

4. Several months after training, administer a focused feedback assessment targeted on the skills being developed. Compare the two sets of scores to determine how much skills have improved.

This approach has significant benefits. First, the results of the pre-course diagnostic allow participants to set quantifiable, performance improvement goals. Also, participants are more focused and motivated when they know there will be a follow-up assessment. The follow-up assessments create accountability. The assessment results show whether the individual has improved performance. You can administer repeat post-course assessments over time to produce ongoing measures of performance improvement.

How 360 Feedback Helped One Manager Get Better Results

"Jacob" was a newly promoted manager with a major utility company. With his new position, he inherited a team of 13 supervisors. Most were long-term employees, and Jacob was much younger than most of his direct reports. Several of the supervisors thought they deserved the promotion and resented his appointment.

Jacob soon discovered that the performance of his supervisors was below par. He spent a lot of time working on relationships with each of them, clarifying service standards and trying to build a cohesive team. Despite his best efforts, Jacob encountered resistance; and performance did not improve. He knew that the supervisors were unhappy, but he couldn't get them to talk about their dissatisfaction. When he learned about the power of 360 feedback, he decided to use it to ask for input about his leadership practices. He hoped that the information gained would provide a basis for dialogue and team building.

With the help of Shauna, a consultant hired to facilitate the process, Jacob selected the behaviors critical to his leadership. Shauna then met with the team and explained how the feedback would be collected, assuring everyone that their responses would be anonymous. After the questionnaires were completed, Shauna met with Jacob to help him interpret the data in the report and establish his priorities for action. She also coached him on how to respond to the feedback with his team.

Over the next few weeks, Jacob met with his direct reports individually and as a group. He asked them to clarify certain aspects of the feedback. He also explained which priority areas he planned to work on first and why he did not plan to alter some behaviors. Jacob saw an immediate change in his team. Resistance decreased, productivity increased and a customer service orientation began to take hold. Over time, he was able to rebuild his team of supervisors. They pulled together to become the only team to meet or exceed all established performance goals for the next quarter. They continued to perform well, and within the year Jacob received a substantial promotion. He attributed much of his success to the 360 feedback process and the open dialogue it produced.

When used correctly, 360 feedback is a powerful tool for increasing awareness about the improvements that colleagues, coworkers, and others would like to see and for engaging in dialogue to discuss opportunities for growth and development as a team member.

The next chapter addresses the individual effort needed to master a skill.

"If we want to hardwire a new behavior, we just need to give our new mental map enough attention, over enough time, to ensure it becomes embedded in our brain. We do this by making links to different parts of the brain so that the web of links thickens and spreads out....If we literally put enough energy into the insight or idea, it will become a part of who we are."

—David Rock

Quiet Leadership

5

The Classic 3 Steps for Mastering Skills

Whether you learn about a more effective way to do something in a learning program, a video, or a book, you'll have work to do to make the improved skill an automatic behavior pattern. This follow-through effort could take many weeks, or even months. The key to all skill-building is practice, practice, and more practice. With each "rep," applying the skill during a demanding work day will get easier.

Even though it can be challenging to change a behavior, if you implement these three steps—*and repeat them often*—you *will* get through the awkward construction phase and establish the new work habit:

1. Focus

2. Action

3. Reflection

Step 1 – FOCUS

When you discover multiple opportunities for development, such as you often see in a 360 feedback report, you may be tempted to set goals to improve several areas at once. This would be a mistake. You can't attack several personal changes simultaneously if you want them to become permanent. Although you may think you can get more done by working on many things at once, actually you'd be spreading yourself too thin. You wouldn't be able to get enough practice in any one area to build new brain circuits.

To permanently change any aspect of behavior as quickly as possible, the key is to stay focused on only one behavior pattern at a time. That's why *focus* is the first step. Focusing means taking a good hard look at yourself and identifying the *one* thing that keeps tripping you up. Then concentrate exclusively on improving that one skill until the new pattern becomes automatic.

If you're not sure what your #1 priority should be, ask the people who know you well. They can see what you can't. They're aware of the behaviors that cause problems for them. Be gracious when you hear the truth about yourself, and thank them for their honesty.

Another aspect of focus is learning how to perform the skill correctly through coaching, demonstrations, books, videos, or other resources. Then concentrate your attention on implementing the *one* behavior that will help you improve.

Step 2 – ACTION

Once you identify what to work on—and find out how to do it right—it's time to *take action:* apply what you've learned in real situations. And not just once or twice. Dozens or even hundreds of times. Remember, you're creating new physical connections in your brain, which takes a lot of repetitions.

The secret is to keep your eyes open for every possible opportunity to use the skill. And when you see the chance, remember baseball star Pablo Sandoval's philosophy: *When you walk up to the plate, swing the bat.* Some players pause too long, waiting for the perfect pitch, and as a result, they miss out on possible hits. Not Sandoval. During his career he understood that the more swings he took, the more likely he would be to hit the ball. He learned that's how you hit a home run, even if it means sometimes striking out in the process.

You can apply this uncomplicated approach when performing a new skill or changing an established habit. Don't allow yourself to be stopped by:

- Fear of failure
- Concerns about criticism from others
- Striving for perfection
- Anxiety about making a mistake

Instead, do the best you can in that moment, in that situation.

Step 3 – REFLECTION

Learning doesn't automatically happen just because you try something. That's why the third step is so vital. You accelerate the learning process when you take time to think about what happened and what you learned from a situation. Making time to reflect allows you to extract lessons that will refine your skill for the next time. If you don't slow down and think about your experiences, you risk repeating the same mistakes and never learning from them. This often happens. People go from one situation to another without taking away the lessons.

So what exactly should you think about? What does "reflection" look like? If you take a few minutes to ask yourself these five questions after you apply a skill, you'll be astonished at the insights you get:

1. **What happened?** How do you feel about it? Who did what? What was the sequence of events?

2. **Why did it happen that way?** Cause and effect? Your motives? What helped or hindered?

3. **What were the consequences?** Outcomes? Benefits? Costs? Problems? Resolutions?

4. **How would you handle a similar situation in the future?** What lessons did you learn? What basic principles?

5. **What are your next steps?** What will you do in the next 48 hours to implement this learning?

For best results, don't just think about your answers. Actually write them down. Your brain analyzes more deeply when you do this, and it will help you remember the lesson. Also, being able to review what you learned will reinforce your learning even more.

Download the worksheet, "Reflection Questions" to review the questions and record your answers after you apply a skill: **https://GrowStrongLeaders.com/bonus**

The reflection process is one of the most powerful tools for letting go of the past and creating a plan for going forward.

How Reflection Helped Me

In 2010 I attended a large conference for entrepreneurs, with more than 1,000 attendees. The night before the official event kicked off, I was able to attend an exclusive reception for just 100 people. It represented a terrific opportunity to meet potential partners and clients.

After most guests had arrived, the host passed around a microphone so each person could give a 30-second introduction. The idea was to say something compelling about your business so those who might be interested in your products and services could seek you out later. I wasn't sure of the best approach; and when my turn did come, I felt like I didn't exude confidence. I didn't grab their attention. Not a single person came up to me afterwards. During the rest of the reception, I spent a lot of time beating myself up for not taking full advantage of the opportunity. Critical thoughts kept running through my mind.

When I got back to my hotel room, I knew I needed to do something to let go of the incident. Otherwise, I'd waste valuable time and energy dwelling on something I couldn't change and feeling bad about myself in the process. I decided to write out the answers to the five Reflection questions. I knew that doing this would force my brain to think about the situation in a different light. I recorded my answers on a notepad. Completing this exercise helped me focus on creating a better outcome in the future. It gave me new insights and helped me move on with more clarity and intention. The endless replays of the earlier scene stopped. I was able to relax and enjoy the event.

An Example from an Executive

A senior-level executive, "Alicia," told me about her experience applying the reflection exercise. She used the questions so often that she memorized them. She formed the habit of analyzing a situation through the filter of these five questions, so she could quickly gain insights for the future.

Alicia also used them to coach her direct reports. She discovered that asking the questions prevented her from jumping in with her opinions and dispensing advice. Instead, she helped people draw out their own "lessons learned." This approach helped them recognize the take-aways and accelerated improvements in performance.

Do the Reps

Completion of these three steps—Focus, Action and Reflection—is what we refer to as a repetition, or "rep," of the desired behavior, just like completing reps of a sport skill. One rep includes:

- **Focus**: Reviewing what to do—how to perform the skill

- **Action**: Applying the behavior in a real-world situation

- **Reflection**: Analyzing the experience to take away lessons for the next repetition

If you repeat this cycle of focus, action and reflection enough times, the enabling circuit will connect and the behavior will become automatic. It takes many reps to reach the ultimate goal: a new, well-established work habit. As with any skill, the key to ingraining it is practice, practice and more practice—a lot of application over time.

In the next chapter, I describe the importance of receiving feedback on an ongoing basis to help you find out what others want and need from you.

"Feedback is the breakfast of
Champions."

— Ken Blanchard

*Author of several classic books on
leadership*

6

Ongoing Focused Feedback

Diagnostic 360 feedback is the best way to identify strengths and areas that need improvement. But this initial effort is not enough. As you attempt to make changes, you also need ongoing focused feedback about your progress.

Several years ago, I needed to see my ophthalmologist about a problem with one of my eyes. My regular doctor wasn't available, so I met with another physician in the practice. When he came into the room, he asked me about my business. I told him that our company has survey software that makes it easy to get feedback from employees and customers. He immediately winced and said with all sincerity, "Gosh, I don't want to know what *they* think!" His response has stuck with me all this time because it's a common reaction people have about receiving input from others.

Feedback is a *gift*.

To measure progress, people need feedback as they are working to ingrain a new skill. But most people dread getting feedback. And for good reason. After all, most of the time it isn't praise, right? It's criticism about some kind of issue. Whether you mean to or not, you're probably doing something that's causing a problem, and now somebody is about to point this out to you. You get a knot in the pit of your stomach. You think, *"Oh great, here it comes..."*

But there's a better approach. What if you adopted a positive attitude and started thinking of feedback as a gift? Yes, a gift. If you're making things difficult for the people around you, there can only be bad consequences; and you won't realize the negative impact of your actions unless someone points it out to you. For your own good, it's important to have this mirror held up to your behavior.

It's likely that people are reluctant to approach you about your behavior. After all, nobody wants to be the bearer of bad news. Why? Because they may think you don't want to hear it or that you'll get defensive or angry. Plus, they may not know the best way to give feedback. If they did, they might feel more confident about giving it.

So when someone does come to you with feedback, adjust your attitude. Recognize that what they're saying represents a valuable offering that can have long-term benefits for you and your relationship. It took courage for the person to approach you with this information, so welcome it and do everything you can to encourage more of it. Focus on the good you're going to get from it. You'll discover what everyone else already knows: the problem behaviors in your blind spot. Don't frame the feedback as a judgment of your faults. Think of it as ideas that can help you become the best version of yourself.

My husband pointed out one of my blind spots.

My husband Lee and I were in the kitchen preparing dinner, and I said, "I'm thinking that broccoli would be great as a side dish."

He looked at me and chuckled.

"What are you laughing about?"

"It's just that you've been starting a lot of sentences lately with 'I'm thinking...' and I bet you don't even realize you're doing it."

I had no clue. I was completely unaware that I was even saying those words. Until he pointed it out to me.

"Does it bother you?" I asked.

"Well, yes, because I get distracted by the number of times you say it. Then it's hard to pay attention to the rest of what you're saying."

At first, I thought he was being picky, and then I remembered something similar that I'd experienced recently at a picnic with members of a local club. I was sitting next to a man I'd met before but had not spoken with much. I asked him questions to learn more about his life, and he ended almost every sentence with *"...you know what I mean?"* He didn't wait for me to respond yes or no. It was more of a rhetorical question. But I did find his constant use of it distracting. I actually found myself anticipating that phrase and missing some of the words that came before.

As I recalled that situation, my annoyance with Lee's comment became a learning moment for me. I could honestly tell him that I *appreciated* his letting me know about my habit and that I'd work on changing it. Now it's become a source of amusement for us, because when I forget and use the phrase, I catch myself, laugh, and change it to something else. And sometimes Lee will start a sentence with, "I'm thinking..." and I'll smile and say, "Oh, you are?" And we immediately laugh about it. Now we're catching each other because he picked up the phrase from me!

The truth is, we all have blind spots, words we say or actions we take that have a negative impact on someone else. Sometimes it's minor, like the above situations. But sometimes it's major, like saying hurtful, thoughtless things to another person and not being aware of the pain that the words inflict. Or using a condescending tone when you're convinced you're right and others don't know what they're talking about. Or expressing exasperation with a coworker, a customer or even your child, and not realizing that your reaction had the opposite effect from what you intended.

The best solution to dissolving blind spots is to make sure you have people in your life who are willing to speak up and tell you the truth about your behavior. If you can't think of anyone like that, I invite you to look within and ask why that's the case.

Receiving Constructive Feedback

To get the kind of feedback you need to measure your progress, you need to ask for and respond to the feedback graciously. Think back to a time when someone approached you about something you said or did that created a problem. *How did you respond?*

It's natural to feel defensive or even angry when you hear feedback that's different from the way you see yourself. But if you react with defensiveness or anger, you push the other person away and discourage future feedback. In the process, you rob yourself of valuable information and risk damaging the relationship. Remember that when people talk to you about your blind spots, it's because they care enough about you and the relationship to risk holding up a mirror so you can see yourself as they see you.

To receive feedback graciously so you can perform at your best, incorporate these important elements in your approach and response:

Ask for feedback. Actively seek input from people who know your strengths and areas for development first-hand and you trust will be honest with you. Acknowledge that you recognize there's room for improvement and you want to do better. Explain that you need their help to focus on what matters and get it right. Ask them to be specific when describing what they've observed. Then tell them you'd like their support, because changing your habitual way of doing things will take time.

Listen without defensiveness. After asking for feedback, you can actually blow it in a single moment. That's what could happen if you heard something that made you uncomfortable and you tried to justify or defend your actions. The key is to silently recognize what you're feeling and *say nothing*. Just focus on listening well. Check what you believe you're hearing to be sure you get it right, and ask questions to clarify what they would like you to do going forward.

Acknowledge your mistakes. When you do this, you'll send the clear message that you really *get* what they're trying to say, that they made the right choice to tell you.

Thank them. Expressing your appreciation to those who took a risk to give you feedback makes it safe for them to approach you in the future.

Apologize. World-renowned executive coach and author Marshall Goldsmith calls this *the magic move*. It's magic because if you do this in a genuine way, your credibility with those individuals increases dramatically and your relationship can advance to a whole new level. Apologizing tells them you own up to your mistakes.

Commit. Let them know you're motivated and committed to making improvements. That's the response people hope for when they decide to give you feedback.

Follow up. It's important to stay in touch after someone gives you feedback about a specific behavior. You can help them replace their old images of you with new ones by telling them about your progress. Let them know you're continuing to make an effort. From time to time, ask them, *"How am I doing?"* and *"What one or two suggestions do you have for me to get even better?"*

One Owner's Transformation after Constructive Feedback

"Jeff" owns a hotel in the Northeast. A few years ago he was distressed about problems with his staff. There was a lot of absenteeism, and morale seemed quite low. He knew he wasn't getting the best from the managers and employees, but he didn't know why. He asked a consultant to set up an employee opinion survey. Jeff thought people would give honest input if they knew their responses would be anonymous and confidential. He was right. The results stunned him. In fact, the feedback was a huge "wake-up call" that dramatically changed the way he viewed his team and ran his business.

One of Jeff's core values is treating people with respect. But the survey showed that people disliked coming to work because of the oppressive, controlling environment he'd created. Jeff was shocked to learn there was a huge gap between the culture he wanted and the one he'd actually created. *Before doing this survey, he had no idea that people felt this way!*

The good news is that Jeff used this information to think about what the staff really needed from him. He asked the consultant to serve as his coach as he worked on changing his management style. Six months later, when this consultant walked into the hotel, she immediately sensed a difference in the attitudes of the people she encountered. They said that they loved coming to work now because the atmosphere at the hotel was totally transformed. Jeff was listening more and commanding less. When she walked into Jeff's office, he was beaming. He thanked her for the role she and the survey results had played in changing his life. Not only had he modified his behavior at work and improved his relationship with everyone there, his changes also had a profound impact on his relationship with his family.

I spoke to this consultant a few years after the original survey, and she shared that Jeff has continued to make improvements. He conducts surveys on a regular basis now to make sure he's on track with his behavior.

Jeff did several things right:

1. **He had the courage to ask for feedback.** Many of us would prefer not to know the truth or we're afraid of what we might hear, so we avoid asking.

2. **He was brutally honest with himself and took responsibility for his actions.** He didn't react defensively, make excuses, or try to justify his behavior.

3. **He made a commitment to change and then followed through.** Sometimes we recognize that we need to change, but we never get around to doing anything about it.

4. **He asked for assistance while making the changes.** He realized that a coach could reduce his learning curve and provide the support he needed.

You don't have to use a formal survey process to get feedback from the people who are important to you. Just commit to asking at least three people this one question:

---

*"What one thing could I do better that would
make the biggest difference in our relationship?"*

If people sense that you genuinely want to know so you can make improvements in your behavior, you will get insights that can help you make changes that strengthen all of your relationships.

Receiving Positive Feedback

As part of measuring your progress, positive feedback is just as important as constructive feedback. While this chapter has focused primarily on receiving *constructive* feedback, it wouldn't be complete without addressing the skill of receiving *positive* feedback, too. That's because most people haven't been taught how to do it. Too often, there's a tendency to discount or minimize what someone is saying when they pay us a compliment. We might be tempted to say, "Oh, it was nothing" or "No big deal." The problem with this type of response is that it judges the other person's perspective and conveys that their opinion is invalid or incorrect.

When another person takes time to praise something you said or did, you can be gracious and simply say, "Thank you for noticing and mentioning that. I really appreciate it."

In addition to receiving diagnostic 360 feedback and ongoing focused feedback, you can accelerate development by working with a coach. That's the focus of the next chapter.

Access short video tips that help you strengthen your skills for expressing appreciation, apologizing, offering encouragement, and listening:
https://GrowStrongLeaders.com/Bonus

"Coaching can fuel the courage to step out beyond the comfortable and familiar, can help people learn from their experiences and can literally and metaphorically increase and help fulfill a person's potential."

– Michael Bungay Stanier

The Coaching Habit: Say Less, Ask More & Change the Way You Lead Forever

7

Why Coaching Is Essential

Professional athletes in individual sports like golf and tennis continuously invest in coaches who show them ways to take their game to the next level. Then they follow through, applying what they learn over and over, getting feedback during practice and analyzing how to improve in the next competition. This process takes time, but it's a critical component for helping athletes make lasting improvements in their performance.

In a corporate setting, leaders and team members need coaching for exactly the same reasons. When done well, coaching is vital to sustaining confidence, improving skills, and making long-term changes in behavior.

What Coaching IS and IS NOT

Before discussing how you can make the best use of coaches in your organization, let's take a quick look at how coaching is different from other types of interventions.

Therapy. When you work with a therapist, you're often focused on resolving issues that occurred *in the past* that are interfering with functioning effectively in the present. Coaching, on the other hand, is *future-focused*. The coach helps you identify opportunities for development and create an actionable strategy for achieving specific goals.

Mentoring. A mentor is a seasoned professional who takes an advisory role and provides less experienced professionals with guidance based on acquired wisdom and experience. While coaching could be an aspect of what a mentor provides, the actual coaching process is not focused on advising or directing. Instead, the coach helps you form your own goals and development plan.

Consulting. Organizations hire consultants with expertise in a specific area. The consultant typically assesses, analyzes data, offers recommendations and even assists with implementation. Coaching is less directive and more supportive. The coach uses a discovery-based approach, asking questions that help you identify the focus of your work together.

Training. A set curriculum is designed to help participants learn about specific skills. The course instructor has established objectives, usually set out in a linear path, and the teaching process occurs within a structured event. Coaching is not an event. The coach meets with you at agreed-upon timeframes where you evaluate progress and adjust your goals.

Disciplinary Action. If an organization brings in a coach to salvage a leader on the brink of being fired, a stigma can be associated with the coaching process. Instead, coaching is most effective when used as a standard development tool, demonstrating the organization's commitment to investing in its talent.

What does a coach actually *do*?

If you've never worked with a coach, you may be wondering what the engagement looks like. Coaches typically start by identifying where you are now. They may have you complete assessments that reveal information about your behavior style, personality or values. They may also conduct in-person or automated 360 behavior feedback surveys (see Chapter 4) to determine what your stakeholders perceive to be your greatest strengths and development opportunities.

With that information in hand, together you and your coach determine the primary areas of focus in your work together. Then during your sessions, these are some of the actions your coach will take:

- Ask questions designed to make you think and draw out your own answers

- Listen deeply for what is said and not said

- Demonstrate curiosity

- Challenge you to be honest with yourself and identify limiting beliefs that may be holding you back

- Guide you to take a different approach in areas that are causing you problems

- Assist you in breaking unhelpful habits/behavior patterns that are getting in your way

- Hold you accountable for fulfilling your commitments

The length of the engagement varies. If the coach is to help someone actually make *long-term* changes in behavior patterns, a minimum of 6-12 months is typical.

Benefits of Having a Coach

When you work with a skilled coach, you increase the odds that you'll make real improvements in your performance over time. Coaching is not intended to be a quick fix.

These are some of the benefits you can expect to see:

- Increased self-awareness and self-confidence

- Healthier, happier relationships at work and at home

- Greater effectiveness in handling challenging situations

- Reduced stress and feelings of overwhelm

- Greater balance and inner calm

Experiencing these payoffs depends not just on the coach's ability. You must take responsibility for fulfilling your commitments if you want to make real progress.

Who Needs Coaching?

The fact is, *everyone* needs coaching.

Companies often hire executive coaches for C-suite leaders. Sometimes they invest in coaches for the next level of leaders, too. Or they might opt to have selected employees get certified so they can serve as internal coaches for groups like mid-level managers.

So far, it's been rare for organizations to invest in coaches for supervisors and team contributors or to teach people how to coach each other as they work together. To improve the performance of *every* person, you're wise to focus on creating a *coaching culture* that starts at the top and cascades through all levels of your organization.

One-on-One Coaching for Executives

Whether your organization is large or small, it's often lonely at the top. For a variety of reasons, senior leaders often don't recognize when they are the source of problems and their direct reports may be hesitant to speak up. This means the owner or CEO ends up with blind spots that could cause all kinds of issues throughout the company.

Bringing in an executive coach can accelerate the resolution of these situations. The objective, detached perspective of an outsider can be essential to the executive acknowledging the problem and committing to solve it. The ultimate goal is to create an atmosphere where everyone thrives. In the process of being coached, senior leaders learn how to become better coaches themselves. When this happens, executive coaches can consciously and intentionally begin the process of setting up a coaching culture throughout the organization.

Group Coaching for Managers

While it may be cost-prohibitive to have a coach work individually with managers, there's an economical alternative that works well.

If managers have attended a leadership skills class, you can divide them into small groups of 5-8 to continue working together afterwards. An internal or external coach can meet with them once or twice a month so they can discuss progress and hold each other accountable. Depending on where participants work, these sessions can be facilitated in-person or virtually via an online meeting platform.

The facilitator uses coaching skills such as asking open-ended questions, listening deeply, and displaying curiosity. In this setting, participants learn more about effective ways to coach their respective team members in addition to improving their own performance around the topic being studied and practiced. If budget permits, you could include one-on-one sessions with the coach periodically, such as once per quarter, to privately discuss individual issues or questions.

You can be creative about structuring group coaching, incorporating suggestions described in the next chapter on support systems.

Peer Coaching for All Levels

Today there are technology platforms that facilitate *peer* coaching, which makes coaching accessible to everyone. Participants not only study content to develop the skill they want to improve, they also communicate their progress to their cohort. When done well, this type of coaching has the potential to produce transformational results.

The beauty of this approach is that you don't have to use an outside paid professional coach (although this is an option). Instead, the person who serves as the primary peer coach can be an internal person who has basic coaching skills and is committed to the success of the participants. The coach could be a participant's manager, someone in Human Resources or Talent Development, coworkers, or any internal champion who wants to help develop a coaching culture throughout the organization.

In one case where a manager used the *Strong for Performance* platform for professional development, "Carla" received coaching from an internal coach, a professional from HR. First, Carla used the program to seek input from her direct reports to help her select the skill to focus on. She shared the results with her coach, and together they identified "Engaging in Dialogue" as the communications skill to improve. Carla acknowledged that in the past, she would cut off supervisors who came to her with concerns or complaints about a situation. She wasn't interested in hearing their opinions or the reasoning behind them. She was always in a hurry and wanted to get through these exchanges as quickly as possible so she could get back to the task at hand.

Carla followed the Focus-Action-Reflection approach described in Chapter 5. She studied the material related to dialogue, committed to specific actions, and sent the plan to her coach. After applying the skill with a member of her team, she answered reflection questions about what happened, why it happened that way, the consequences, and how she'd handle future situations. She then shared these responses with her coach. In turn, the coach replied with feedback and suggestions that would be useful to Carla going forward. These types of ongoing exchanges provided encouragement for Carla as she tried new ways of interacting with her staff.

As she came to appreciate the importance of listening and seeking to understand what was behind another person's thinking, Carla decided to slow down. She started taking more time to hear a person out. She made a conscious effort with one individual in particular whom she'd judged in the past as a "complainer." On one occasion, Carla asked him to tell her more about his concerns and his ideas for resolving the problem. To her surprise, Carla discovered information she'd not previously known. It changed the way she viewed the situation *and* this supervisor. As a result of their conversation, Carla reversed a decision she'd previously been adamant about, and she announced this to her entire team.

As she continued to use dialogue skills and demonstrate a genuine interest in understanding the opinions of others, Carla dramatically altered the tone and feel of her office. People communicated more openly not just with her, but with each other, as they felt their ideas were now respected and appreciated.

The Importance of Accountability

Most of us are more motivated to follow through when we know someone will be checking up on us. We need to be held accountable. And this is a *good* thing.

---

*"...and accountable has no sense of blame. It means, **count on me**." – Dusan Djukich, Straight-Line Leadership*

One of the most important drivers in performance improvement is knowing we'll need to answer to our coach about the actions we've taken since our last conversation. This also holds true for the coaches themselves.

For years, Marshall Goldsmith has had his own accountability coach who contacts him at the same time *every day*. The coach asks him several questions that Marshall himself created. These questions serve to keep Marshall on track as he goes through his day, because he's keenly aware of the answers he'll have to give later when he's asked:

- *How much walking did you do?*

- *How many hours of sleep did you get?*

- *How much time did you spend writing?*

- *How many times did you try to prove you were right when it wasn't worth it?*

My Own Accountability Coach

A common thread in this book is the notion that it's all too easy to attend a training course, workshop or conference, get excited about what you learn, and then have nothing change afterwards. That has happened to me. I've attended programs, taken copious notes, and then gotten caught up in my day-to-day tasks after returning to the office. The good intentions fade, and the pages of notes get filed away.

After making a significant investment in a week-long business development workshop in mid-2019, I was determined that this time would be different. Another participant and I agreed to be accountability partners with each other. Ever since, we've had a call every other Monday morning for one hour. It's a structured time with each of us having 30 minutes to discuss:

1. Our wins since the last call

2. Review of our commitments from the previous week and whether or not we completed them. If not, what did we work on instead?

3. New commitments for the coming week

4. Any help or ideas we feel we need from the other person

Knowing that I'll be answering to this person every 14 days has helped me stay focused and more engaged with my priorities. I can count on her to cheer me on for my successes and ask me the hard questions if I try to let myself off the hook.

Any pair or small group of people in an organization can set up this kind of accountability with each other. The creativity, synergy and outcomes that emerge can be remarkable.

Manager As Coach

While there are programs available that teach managers how to take on the role of "coach," there are a few key things they need to start doing in order to immediately shift from being directive or advising. As coach, the goal is to help others *discover their own answers*. Just as parents need to learn this approach when preparing their teens for life away from home, leaders are most effective when they take time to facilitate team members figuring out things for themselves.

Here are three steps they can take:

1. **Assume an attitude of *curiosity*.** We often feel time-starved, so we're typically focused on our own priorities. Making the effort to notice when someone else seems upset or just needs to talk is a first step. A simple acknowledgement and an invitation can provide an opportunity to learn important information and be of service to the other person at the same time.

   "You seem upset. Want to talk about it?"

   "I can tell you're not your normal cheerful self. What's going on?"

   "Can I be of help in some way?

2. **Use *deep listening*.** When we're listening effectively in a coaching role, we aren't passive. We're paying attention to the words and tone of voice, and we're noticing the other person's body language as they speak. We check what we think we understand. Being in the presence of a powerful listener is such a rare thing that people feel affirmed and validated by the experience. We can form a powerful connection when we communicate through our own body language that

we're fully present and that this individual is the most important person in our world at this moment.

3. **Ask *open-ended* questions.** Avoid starting questions with "Why" as that word—no matter what follows after it—sounds like a judgment and can put others on the defensive.

Instead, start questions with *"What"*...

- *What do you think is the real issue?*

- *What do you think might be a better way?*

- *What might happen if you choose Option A? Option B?*

- *What's caused you to draw that conclusion?*

- *What do you need from me in order to make that happen?*

- *What would you like to do next?*

- *What would support look like?*

Or *"How"*...

- *How do you feel about what happened?*

- *How do you think it would turn out if you took that approach?*

- *How could you look at this in a different way so you could see other possible solutions?*

- *How could I best help you in this situation?*

Notice that none of these questions can be answered with a simple word or two. They get a person to talk, to do the kind of thinking that will lead to learning and action. The key is for managers to recognize when they need to operate in the coaching role and watch for opportunities to use these steps.

Creating a Coaching Culture

As leaders at all levels begin to implement these three behaviors—curiosity, listening, and questioning—they model coaching for all employees. The goal is to have people become comfortable *coaching each other* as the need arises.

Creating a coaching culture simply means helping employees learn a few new skills for doing this. Such a culture emphasizes regular feedback and opportunities for growth, creating a more engaged and energized workforce. Other elements addressed in this book—accountability, giving and receiving feedback, providing support to others, engaging core strengths—all contribute to the establishment of a strong performance improvement culture.

In the next chapter, you'll find out why it's important to have a larger support system beyond a single coach.

"Good listeners are like trampolines:
You can bounce ideas off of them, and
rather than absorbing your ideas and
energy, they amplify, energize, and
clarify your thinking. They make you
feel better not by merely passively
absorbing, but by actively supporting.
This lets you gain energy and height,
just like a trampoline."

— Jack Zenger and Joseph Folkman

"What Great Listeners Actually Do" in
Emotional Intelligence: Empathy

8

The Role of a Support System

Changing a behavior pattern takes work. Along the way, you can get discouraged and want to give up as you experience setbacks or failures. It helps immensely to have the active support of others who...

- Care enough to make regular contact

- Hold you accountable

- Encourage you to stay the course

- Can be trusted to keep what is said confidential

A built-in support system is a key reason why 12-step programs and Weight Watchers have been so successful for decades. To achieve their goals, participants need to make changes to ingrained lifestyle habits. The support of a sponsor and other caring individuals helps them stay on track as they work to adopt new behavior patterns.

Belief

You have to *believe* that you're capable of making the change, that it's possible for *you*. This may sound simple, but it's not. We all carry baggage related to our capabilities, much of it inaccurate. In *The Power of Habit*, author Charles Duhigg points out the importance of a support group, such as AA, in expanding one's beliefs. He shares this insight from Lee Ann Kaskutas, a senior scientist at the Alcohol Research Group:

"There's something really powerful about groups and shared experiences. People might be skeptical about their ability to change if they're by themselves, but a group will convince them to suspend disbelief. A community creates belief."

In addition to having an accountability coach, you'll benefit from having other support coaches who care about your professional success as you work on your development. These individuals could be a mix of:

- Managers
- Co-workers
- Training class instructor and co-participants
- Mentors
- Colleagues in other organizations
- Friends
- Family members

Let's take a closer look at one valuable skill these coaches can use to provide an effective support system.

Encouragement

Initial attempts to change a behavior can be discouraging. Old habits kick in automatically, and it takes a conscious effort to try something different. Even if someone remembers to try the new way, their initial efforts may not get the results they hoped for. This can be so disheartening that a person loses sight of what's possible and is tempted to stop trying. This is the "crunch point" I've referred to. This is where a coach's encouragement comes in.

These are the four steps involved in becoming a strong encourager.

1. **Listen.** It's important to take time to understand more about the situation and the person's feelings. Listening allows us to learn why people feel discouraged. This is not the time to give advice, criticize, or try to reason with them.

2. **Affirm.** This is an opportunity to remind them of their strong qualities and obstacles they've faced before in equally tough or even tougher situations and what they did to succeed. Affirming highlights the positives, which strengthens their belief that they have the capability to work through the current challenge.

3. **Offer perspective.** When they're discouraged, people are focused on the negatives about the situation, which is a natural reaction. A support coach acknowledges the difficulty of what they're doing, then restores a balanced, realistic perspective by reminding them of the advantages and opportunities. Pointing out the positives is helpful, because the upsides are as real as the downsides.

4. **Offer support.** When people are in a bad place, they often feel alone. They feel the weight of the situation and think they have to handle everything themselves. Coaches let them know others are there for them and care about their well-being and success. They ask questions like, *"What do you need from me now? What would support look like to you?"*

The idea is to help people to stick with it. To change a behavior pattern, they need to keep trying, even though the early going is rough. The more often they make a conscious effort, the easier it will get.

Encouragement in Action

I vividly remember a time when I needed encouragement at work. One of my business partners, Paula, was out on extended medical leave. I absorbed most of her responsibilities during those two months. At times I found myself getting anxious and discouraged from the additional pressures. My other partner, Denny, works in another state and couldn't help with most of these day-to-day tasks. But he was my encourager.

One day, when I was feeling really overwhelmed, I told Denny how hard it was to juggle everything. He asked me to talk about what was bothering me, and then he listened without once interrupting or jumping in with advice. When I finished unloading, he acknowledged that what I was doing was hard. He reminded me of some times in the past when I had excelled despite some really tough circumstances. Denny also affirmed my core strengths and reassured me that in the end I'd be able to get everything done. Then he made this suggestion: "It's true that the last eight weeks have been just as hard as you say. But instead of focusing on the past, try shifting your perspective to the future. You know Paula will be back in a week or so. Think about that and how great it will be."

This simple conversation helped change my outlook. I felt like a new person when I went home that day. I had my confidence back. And I thought how great it was to have a partner who knows how to encourage.

You can also use these steps when you need to encourage someone on your team. A caring community can go a long way to shore up resolve and keep people on track when they're working on self-improvement. Whether it's just one other person or dozens of individuals, these supporters can play a key role in strengthening belief, motivation and commitment.

Feedback, learning, coaching and support play vital roles as you work to improve a skill. The next chapter addresses an element that's critical to making all the others work.

Access short video tips I recorded to help you develop skills for supporting others, such as listening, expressing appreciation, apologizing and offering encouragement: **https://GrowStrongLeaders.com/Bonus**

"Strength does not come from winning. Your struggles develop your strengths. When you go through hardships and decide not to surrender, that is strength."

—Stephen Covey

The 7 Habits of Highly Effective People

9

Addressing Core Strengths

The interactions of a leader with the team and of team members with each other are absolutely crucial to high levels of performance. And the foundation for these interactions is the ability to communicate effectively, which boils down to a handful of priority skills:

- Listen to understand
- Guide learning
- Coach people to think
- Get agreement about expectations
- Offer encouragement
- Express appreciation
- Give feedback constructively
- Accept feedback graciously
- Engage in dialogue
- Resolve conflict creatively

Beyond this skillset, there's another aspect of performance so important that if you don't work on optimizing it, the chances for achieving outstanding results are greatly diminished. You may *want* to make a change and have all the pieces in place—coaching, a support system, feedback—but if you're missing this element, the others may not be able to make up the difference.

This ingredient is *core strengths.* If you're not equipped to deal with the inevitable roadblocks and setbacks that come your way as you work to improve a skill, you won't get the results you hope for.

Core strengths are the behavior patterns required for doing the hard things when dealing with challenges, facing adversity, and creating change.

These strengths are more than passive qualities or virtues. They're *observable behavior patterns.* They're something people can see you do—not just once, but most of the time. It's how you usually act in a given situation.

While there are dozens of core strengths, I'll focus on six that apply to professional development and then describe how the hotel owner Jeff (Chapter 6) engaged each strength as he worked to improve his leadership skills.

Courage

Venturing into unknown territory, such as designing a new product line, pursuing a new market, or conducting an employee engagement survey, can seem scary. You're not sure what you might encounter, and you're not guaranteed positive results.

It's tempting to stick with what's familiar and comfortable. That way, you're less likely to make mistakes. Maybe you believe it's better not to take risks when the outcome is uncertain.

Jeff could have continued operating his hotel as he had been. But he was eager to find out why he was experiencing issues with employee morale and absenteeism. He recognized that the only way to discover the truth was to *ask*, no matter what the answer would be. He overcame his fears and concerns about the possible negative outcomes in order to get at the truth.

Open-mindedness

If you want to get smarter as you move forward in your career and if you want your decisions to be based on the best information, it's important to seek ideas from others and keep an open mind.

It's not easy to hear or accept another person's point of view because it may contradict one of your strongly held beliefs. If a belief means a lot to you, you may be tempted to reject anything that challenges it. To expand your knowledge and improve your performance, you've got to be willing to entertain perspectives that differ from your own.

Jeff could have gotten defensive or blown off the survey results that pointed to his behavior as a key cause of the personnel problems. Instead, he demonstrated curiosity. He moved past the shock of the unexpected feedback to learn what it was that his team needed from him. He kept an open mind about adopting behaviors that represented an overhaul in his current approach.

Accountability

People respect someone who stands up and "faces the music." They believe anyone who does so will probably deal honestly with them and can be trusted. They don't expect you to be perfect.

When you make a mistake or say and do something that negatively impacts others, the best approach is to own up to the part you played. The faster you admit that something is your fault, the faster others will recognize your strength, get over the incident and move on. Apologizing and making amends actually *increases* others' respect for you.

One of the reasons Jeff was able to transform the culture of his company so quickly is because of his willingness to be accountable. Instead of making excuses or pointing the finger at someone else, he accepted ownership for the oppressive environment he'd fostered with his attitude and actions. He apologized to the employees and was able to get them involved in creating solutions.

Commitment

It's possible to jump into something without fully understanding the dedication and resolve required to be successful, whether it's pursuing a degree, starting a new job, getting married, or joining a weight loss program. You may not anticipate the rough spots. Or you may be hesitant to commit because you're not sure you'll be able to deliver on your promises.

The solution is to get involved with your eyes open. Find out what a goal will require of you. Recognize that you may have to invest time and other resources along the way.

Jeff made his commitment public. When he acknowledged his mistakes, he also promised to make improvements. He knew his employees would be watching to see if he followed through. This created a resolve that kept him going even when he made mistakes.

Effort

It's amazing what you can get done when you push yourself to your limits. Sometimes success depends on your willingness to move faster, devote more personal energy, work longer hours, and inspire the same level of effort from your team members.

Good results usually follow from hard work, but they often don't show up right away. You might wonder whether the results you hope for are worth the mental fatigue that you're experiencing along the way. You might wish you didn't have to try so hard.

With his behavior-change plan mapped out, Jeff showed up every day ready to work his plan. He was willing to put in the effort to create the changes he wanted to see in himself and in everyone working in the hotel. His determination to improve was visible to all and had a dramatic impact on the culture over time.

Perseverance

After you make a commitment and put forth the initial effort, challenges can slow your progress. You're likely to face setbacks and disappointments as you work to adopt new ways of thinking and doing. Even if you make a conscious effort, the skill may feel awkward and ineffective. Almost everyone experiences this frustration at some point, because your established habits get in the way of the new habits you're trying to adopt. You could become discouraged and conclude it's not going to work out.

The key is to persist past this "crunch point." If you don't give up, if you keep at it, you'll forget less often. Your efforts will start to achieve results. Keep trying and eventually your "failure rate" will approach zero. As the brain cells connect and insulate, the new habit will get easier. Eventually it will become dominant, and you'll find yourself performing the new, improved skill without consciously deciding to do it.

Jeff did encounter setbacks as he worked to make changes in his style. He slipped into his old habit of micro-managing at times. Instead of giving up, he kept practicing until eventually he became comfortable allowing others to make decisions and take actions without his presence or approval.

At the Core of Your Abilities

Dozens of other core strengths come into play at work, such as composure, decisiveness, excellence, honesty, integrity, initiative, self-discipline and trust. These strengths are so fundamental to success that they lie at the center of all the possible layers of ability, shown in this model.

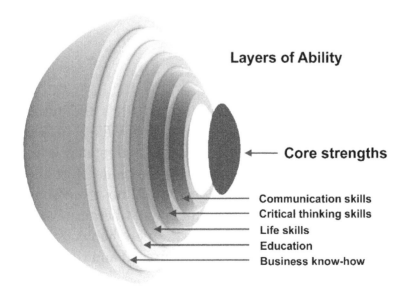

Layers of Ability

← **Core strengths**

Communication skills
Critical thinking skills
Life skills
Education
Business know-how

To effectively perform the actions related to each of the other layers, you'll need to engage core strengths. Here are some things to consider about core strengths:

- **Core strengths are poorly understood.** The notion of "character strength" has always been a foggy one, and it has never been understood as a crucial element of workplace performance. Consequently, it's never been recognized as something you can develop in leaders and high-performing employees.

- **Of all the elements of performance, core strengths probably have the greatest impact.** "Who you are" really is that significant. Imagine someone who lacked business know-how but was strong in most aspects of core strength. Lack of business know-how can be remedied and expertise can be developed in a relatively short period of time. But the consequences of deficits in core strength are enormous.

- **Core strengths are needed for a successful coaching culture.** An environment where people feel safe coaching each other requires that each person exhibits courage, honesty, trust, open-mindedness and cooperation.

- **Core strengths can be developed.** For many people, some strengths are developed in youth. This kind of development can and should continue indefinitely, using opportunities to strive against adversity and learn from these experiences. Leaders can set an example, get agreement about expectations, hold people accountable, and give feedback and encouragement.

Because core strengths are behavior patterns, people can improve them over time. As you work directly on improving a skill and engage strengths like awareness, initiative and perseverance, you'll expand your capacity to use them in other situations.

Access short video tips to help you develop core strengths like courage, focus, composure and self-discipline:
https://GrowStrongLeaders.com/Bonus

"As human beings, we ordinarily go with the obvious. We fall into the habit of relying on behaviors that seem to have worked best for us over the years. We don't readily relinquish that habit pattern. We resist new maneuvers because they make us feel clumsy, awkward, and more at risk. But if you want to accelerate your rate of achievement rapidly, you must search out and vigorously employ new behaviors."

—Price Pritchett, Ph.D.

You²

10
Putting It All Together

The amount of money—billions of dollars annually—wasted on learning and development programs that don't create change is simply outrageous.

My company is on a mission to turn this trend around. The purpose of this book has been to lay out the facts about *why* this has been happening and map out what you can do differently to get better results.

Learning about leader and team skills can be an excellent beginning, but it's only the beginning. If you want your program participants to consistently apply the best practices, they need to repeat the skills in the workplace over and over for months afterward. As we've seen, this is because work habits are ingrained only after persistent repetition.

Yes, there are the rare individuals—the self-motivated high-performers and life-long learners—who are so obsessed with achievement and success that they coach themselves. They perform the desired behaviors on the job and keep after it in spite of setbacks and frustration until they ultimately master the skills, whether there is an adequate follow-through plan in place or not.

In most cases, though, participants will need to incorporate the components described in Chapters 4-9 during the journey towards "unconscious competence."

The Components in Review

Diagnostic 360 Feedback. To target limited resources for development, you need to identify people's strengths and areas for improvement. Asking for input from stakeholders at the beginning of a period of development and then again several months later enables you and participants to measure improvement.

Three Steps for Mastering Skills. It takes a lot of practice to rewire the brain for a new skill. Repeating the cycle of focus, action and reflection enables the circuits to connect and the behavior to become automatic. The result of this process: a new, well-established work habit.

Ongoing Focused Feedback. This practice is essential for tracking people's progress in the areas they're working to improve. In a coaching culture, they are comfortable asking for and graciously accepting constructive feedback.

Coaching. Whether it's an external professional, the person's boss, or a peer, the coaches ask questions, challenge thinking, encourage and hold people accountable for following through on agreements.

Support System. The organization needs a structure that empowers people to reinforce what they're learning and encourage each other to achieve the desired changes. This structure can be supported by technology.

Core Strengths. Working to improve core strengths like courage and perseverance is essential to sticking with skill development, so that people overcome challenges and setbacks along the way.

Creating a Coaching Culture

These components combine to produce an environment that motivates people to perform at their best. When team members receive coaching from their boss or peers, they learn to apply these skills with each other. When an organization has a healthy coaching culture, leaders and team contributors alike:

- Learn basic communication skills for coaching each other

- Demonstrate curiosity and listen to each other with an open mind

- Ask questions that help another person solve a problem or analyze a mistake

- Feel safe being honest with each other, providing both positive and constructive feedback as needed

- Look for ways to support their manager, co-workers and anyone else at any level

- Waste less time dealing with conflicts and the underlying tensions that go with them

- Resolve issues more quickly, so they have more time to be productive

- Do the hard things necessary to achieve an ambitious goal or work through a difficult situation

Closing Questions

No matter what tools you use in addressing the training-performance gap, I invite you to evaluate your current learning and development programs and the type of culture you have around feedback and coaching. Answering the questions below will help you identify areas for improvement.

- *What happens after training? Do participants get involved in a structured, supported long-term program to ingrain newly learned skills?*

- *Do you systematically measure performance to find out whether skills have improved several months after training?*

- *Which of the key elements described in this book are already in place and used effectively?*

- *What are you missing that could help your programs achieve the desired results?*

- *What's the #1 step you can take next to improve your outcomes and create a coaching culture?*

The following roadmap illustrates how you can integrate the six components into a system that results in higher levels of performance, engagement, and a coaching culture. You can download a PDF of the roadmap here: **https://GrowStrongLeaders.com/Bonus**

Roadmap for Creating High Performance

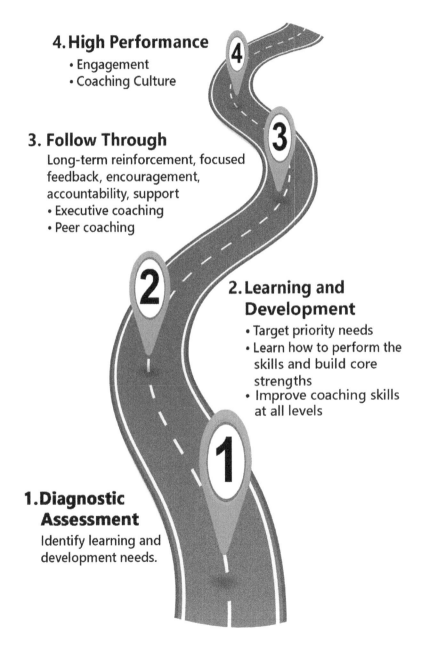

4. High Performance
- Engagement
- Coaching Culture

3. Follow Through
Long-term reinforcement, focused feedback, encouragement, accountability, support
- Executive coaching
- Peer coaching

2. Learning and Development
- Target priority needs
- Learn how to perform the skills and build core strengths
- Improve coaching skills at all levels

1. Diagnostic Assessment
Identify learning and development needs.

Support Tools

Our software company has focused on creating technologies that address the long-standing issues around training and development and the creation of a coaching culture.

If you identified gaps in your current efforts, it's possible one of our programs could provide part of the solution. In that spirit, I'm including a brief overview of them here.

20/20 Insight GOLD – Multi-functional feedback survey tool

Back in the mid- to late-80s, 360-degree feedback was a new concept. The price tag was high, so companies used it primarily for executive development. For respondents, completing the 100+ standard items was a daunting task, and some questions didn't apply to the leaders in that organization. Also, the assessments were cumbersome to administer. Scan forms had to be collected and mailed off for processing.

My business partner Denny Coates and I had a different vision for this technology that involved three criteria:

- **Economical**—Make it feasible for *everyone* to get this type of feedback because we all have blind spots.

- **Customizable**—Make it flexible enough that everyone in the organization can receive diagnostic feedback.

Make it possible to select questions from a vast survey library or add their own locally-developed competencies. Allow customization of other survey elements like scales, respondent types and reports. Include developmental recommendations for every leadership item so participants have suggestions for improving a low-rated skill.

- **User-friendly**—Make the interface intuitive so in-house administrators can quickly and easily set up and run 360 surveys.

When we introduced *20/20 Insight* in 1994, it changed the game for 360 feedback. In fact, the software turned out to be *so* flexible that clients started using it for all kinds of surveys, including customer feedback, opinion, internal quality, team effectiveness and employee engagement. *20/20 Insight* makes it easy to assess the degree to which a company has established a feedback and coaching culture.

Many organizations have done business with us for more than 20 years, and they consistently mention our original three criteria as the key reasons for their loyalty (along with the prompt and exceptional service they receive when contacting us for help).

Strong for Performance – Online reinforcing and coaching platform

---

Based on our years of experience in the assessment and development business, we committed to creating an online technology that facilitated the transition from *knowing* to *doing*. Too many learning systems simply present content with no opportunity for practice and reflection. We incorporated the elements for creating long-term reinforcement of performance into a single program.

The result is *Strong for Performance*, an online development and coaching system. Each participant receives a one-year subscription with 24/7 access to a suite of hundreds of learning resources. Participants can also use the smartphone app. Each subscription includes a copy of the book, *Connect with Your Team: Mastering the Top 10 Relationship Skills.*

Strong for Performance is uniquely suited to support all the components required to create a strong coaching culture.

The program combines the three-step process—Focus, Action, and Reflection—with an accountability coach, support coaching, and the ability to send out one-minute surveys periodically to ask for feedback from stakeholders. Participants can share completed exercises with their coaches to get input, ideas and suggestions. This peer coaching keeps motivation and engagement high, especially when they encounter challenging situations.

Strong for Performance has a vast library of rich content focused on two important topic areas: 40 core strengths and 24 interpersonal skills. Participants can choose from articles, videos and mp3s to get quick tips on how to improve in a specific area.

Sample Topics in Core Strengths

Self-Confidence	Self-Discipline
Composure	Integrity
Initiative	Optimism
Flexibility	Trust

Sample Topics in Interpersonal Skills

Listen to Understand	Express Appreciation
Guide Learning	Give Feedback Constructively
Coach People to Think	Accept Feedback Graciously
Get Buy-in for Expectations	Engage in Dialogue
Offer Encouragement	Resolve Conflict Creatively

You can customize the system for each group of participants, so they access only the content you want them to see. And you can add links to your own custom content.

Clients have used *Strong for Performance* in a variety of ways:

- As a component of a training class
- Post-training follow-up
- Stand-alone tool for development
- Technology support for leadership and peer coaching

Learn more about *20/20 Insight GOLD* and *Strong for Performance* at:
https://GrowStrongLeaders.com

Free Resources
That Will Help You Create a Coaching Culture

Ebooks by Dennis Coates, PhD and Meredith Bell

The Dark Secret of HRD
Coach the People You Care About
Support Coaching
The 5 Secrets to Getting Better at Anything

More Tools

Roadmap for Creating a Coaching Culture
6 Components of a Coaching Culture
Checklist: Is Your Organization Ready for 360 Feedback?
Worksheet: Reflection Questions

Short Videos

Interpersonal Skills	**Core Strengths**
Express appreciation	Courage
Apologize	Composure
Offer encouragement	Focus
Listen	Self-Discipline

Download your free resources at:
https://GrowStrongLeaders.com/bonus

If you found the material in this book helpful, I'd be grateful if you took a few minutes to write a review on Amazon.

When you post a review, it makes a huge difference in helping new readers find my book.

Your review would make my day!

Thank you,
Meredith

References

Baldwin, Timothy and Kevin Ford. "Transfer of Training: A Review and Directions for Future Research" in *Personnel Psychology* (1988).

Brinkerhoff, Robert and Anne Apking, *High Impact Learning: Strategies for Leveraging Business Results from Training* (Basic Books, 2001).

Broad, Mary. *Beyond Transfer of Training: Engaging Systems to Improve Performance* (Pfeiffer, 2005).

Broad, Mary and Jack Phillips. *Transferring Learning to the Workplace* (Association for Talent Development, 1997).

Broad, Mary and John W. Newstrom. *Transfer of Training: Action-Packed Strategies to Ensure High Payoff from Training Investments* (Basic Books, 1992).

Coates, Dennis E. *The Dark Secret of HRD: Four Things You Need to Know to Stop Wasting Money on Training* (First Summit Publishing, 2014).

Kirkpatrick, Donald and James Kirkpatrick. *Transferring Learning to Behavior* (Berrett-Koehler Publishers, 2005).

Kirkpatrick, Donald and Wendy Kayser Kirkpatrick. *Kirkpatrick's Four Levels of Training Evaluation.* (Association for Talent Development, 2016).

Mosel, James. "Why Training Programs Fail to Carry Over," in *Personnel* (1957).

Pfeffer, Jeffrey and Robert I. Sutton. *The Knowing-Doing Gap: How Smart Companies Turn Knowledge into Action* (Harvard Business School Press, 2000).

Pollock, Roy V.H. *et al. The Six Disciplines of Breakthrough Learning, 3rd Edition* (Pfeiffer, 2015).

Acknowledgements

As anyone who's ever written a book knows, it's not a solo project. Others are involved in helping to shape the idea and breathe life into it, suggest resources, case studies or stories that can be used, and offer encouragement or accountability when progress stalls.

I am deeply grateful to my two business partners, Denny Coates and Paula Schlauch. Since 1991, we've worked together to create a company with a stellar reputation and world-class products. I'm honored to be in business with both of them. They have served in every possible role with this book: encourager, editor, accountability coach, proof reader and more. They are two of my best friends in life, and I count myself lucky every day that we made the decision to join forces. Our relationships are based on trust, respect and love that has only deepened over time.

I also want to express appreciation to:

Our clients and resellers, many of whom have worked with us for more than 20 years. The transformational results they've achieved because of our products humbles and inspires me every day.

People who've served as coaches for me through their books, videos, podcasts or personal interactions: Steve Chandler, Steve Hardison, Mark Goulston, Barb Patterson, Jason Goldberg, Robin Sharma, Price Pritchett, Bob Proctor, and Monica DaMaren.

Individuals who've offered encouragement and specific suggestions for this book: Jeri Hetrick, Sharon Weinberg, Angela Cusack, Ben Hipps, Ellen Cooperperson, Shohreh Aftahi, Paul McManus, and Rozanna Wyatt.

My parents, who instilled core strengths in me at a very young age. I strive to live up to the values and principles they modeled throughout their lives.

My husband Lee, who has supported me in this entrepreneurial journey since it started in 1982. He is my rock and my biggest fan.

About the Author

Meredith Bell has been an entrepreneur since 1982, and she's an expert in helping companies develop the *people* side of their business. In her first business as a consultant and trainer, she conducted hundreds of programs for leaders and the members of their teams, helping them communicate and work together more effectively.

Meredith is co-founder and President of Performance Support Systems (PSS), a global software company based in Virginia. Their award-winning assessment and development tools have been used by Fortune 500 companies as well as small-medium size businesses, government agencies, and non-profits to help their leaders and employees identify strengths and opportunities for development. Many clients have done business with PSS for 20+ years.

Meredith has personally worked with thousands of business leaders, Human Resources professionals, Talent and Learning executives, entrepreneurs, consultants, and coaches to assist them in successful implementation of the tools. She is a major content contributor to both *20/20 Insight GOLD* and *Strong for Performance.*

Meredith is the host of the popular Strong for Performance Podcast and is also a frequent guest on podcasts, where she addresses topics like: communications skills for the workplace, the benefits of focusing on giving and being of service, and what's required to develop positive habits and skills over time.

Meredith is available to speak on any of the topics in this book at corporate and association events.

For more information about Meredith:

LinkedIn: https://www.linkedin.com/in/meredithmbell/
Website: https://growstrongleaders.com/
Podcast: https://growstrongleaders.com/podcasts/

Made in the USA
Middletown, DE
08 August 2021

44958593R00066